Wheel

Also by Hayden Saunier

A Cartography of Home
How to Wear This Body
Field Trip to the Underworld (chapbook)
Say Luck
Tips for Domestic Travel

Wheel

Hayden Saunier

Terrapin Books

© 2024 by Hayden Saunier
Printed in the United States of America.
All rights reserved.
No part of this book may be reproduced in any manner,
except for brief quotations embodied in critical articles or reviews.

Terrapin Books
4 Midvale Avenue
West Caldwell, NJ 07006

www.terrapinbooks.com

ISBN: 978-1-947896-74-1
Library of Congress Control Number: 2024932543

First Edition
Redux Series

Cover art by Cheryl Bomba
photograph, *Staying the Course*

Cover design by Diane Lockward

Contents

I
Wheel (1)	7
Falling	8
Here	9
I Go for a Walk While My Cat Eats a Mouse	10
The Way Back	12
Nightfall	13
Some nights I step through different doors	14
Tightening the Trellis	15
Pothole	17
The Story Their Way	18
Proverb	20
As It Is	21
How I Suit Up for Winter Storms	22

II
Dominion	25
Song for a Suburban Mid-Life Crisis	27
Grammar Lesson, Spring 2022	28
Choose Your Filter	29
Epiphany with Book in Hand	30
Lunacy	31
Wheel (2)	32
Weeding After an Argument	34
World in Miniature	35
A Map of the Universe	36
The Uses of Grief	37
Human Interest Story	38
Spell	39

III

Warm Night with Storm and Moon	43
Awake	45
Flight School	46
Digging a Dog's Grave	47
Alchemy	48
Wheel (3)	49
Waters Toward a Sea	50
How This Bee Stuffs Its Pockets	52
Ghazal for Summer Squash	54
Steady	55
Each Year	56
Self-Portrait as Three Cubic Feet of Compost	58

IV

Tricks of the Night Sky	61
The Wisdom Package	62
Some Silences Are Full and Deep as Wells	64
Hidden Systems	65
These Mornings When	66
Ode to the Bird on Edith Wharton's Hat	67
How to Build a Castle	68
Monotype	70
Dear Tea Kettle	71
What I Learned Picking Blackberries at the Farm Dump	72
This Late Thanks	74
Wheel (4)	76

Acknowledgments	79
About the Author	81

The fine—unvarying Axis that regulates the Wheel—

—Emily Dickinson

I

Wheel (1)

There is a *how* to it but not a *why*,
we know enough to know that much, not more,

the way tree roots upturned are birds flown into sky
as if the point is to become what we are not—

we know enough to know that much, not more.
In early spring our footsteps green the path

as if the point is to become ourselves
and then, in time, become an otherness

in early spring. Our footsteps green the path
we walk together through tall woods

which is an otherness we will become in time
while everything around us turns and turns.

We walk together through tall woods
in every season as one rolls into the next

while trees and birds around us turn
and green the path we will become in time.

The point is to become what we are not.
Birds slowly sail through earth; tree roots learn sky.

We know enough to know that much, not more.
There is a *how* to it but not a *why*.

Falling

I fell in love with a field of rye.
It happened this spring for the first time and I am not young.
Let me tell you how this field was both a single being and a multitude.
How it lay open to sky, wind, creature, sound.
How it rippled and flowed, bent, bowed, lay down, arose,
stood tall, grew taller, held its ground.
It hummed and whispered.
Sometimes it went completely still.
I watched it build itself out of nothing but chemistry
in a few short weeks, each stalk forming leaflet, segment,
grain head, braid, fine hairs. As it grew, wild daisies
bloomed inside the long straight rows, each a separate question
to do with love. The sun drove patterns through the furrows,
weaving self and shadow into its warp and woof
and every single color would show, threading stems
with teal, bronze, blue-black, azure, purple, silver-white.
It held the whole world for a while.
And even when the rye was cut down
and lay flat on the earth to dry
where it fell, the all of it
radiated a gold and silver light.
Still, it glowed.

Here

We lie on a grassy bank after lunch,
earth's pitch and angle perfectly fit
to the curves of our backs, hats settled

on faces against a sun that has warmed
the afternoon, coaxed us to stretch out
our bodies, gather heat into bones.

Everything turns into sound. Bird chatter
and shush of leaves still fastened to boughs,
distant droning of highway, that thrum

of so many in motion, and nearby, some small
useful piece of machinery hums. We feel through
our bodies a pulse underneath in the ground

that may or may not be our own. In this drowse,
we become our deep animal selves—more so
than when gulping tin cups of cold water

in hot summer hayfields or desperately
coupled on stairs halfway up, halfway down,
driven hard by blind need—we're just here,

half-asleep in the sun, all brain stem,
intestines, and unstable hearts, on the chance
it's the last warmth for some time to come.

I Go for a Walk While My Cat Eats a Mouse

Or a vole. It's hard to tell which.
I do know it cannot be saved though I didn't

observe the precise moment its life
left its soft, gray, limp body, but sometime

before the equally soft and gray
short-haired domestic American cat

tossed it high through the bright morning air
of my kitchen, his way of checking

for heartbeat, displaying his skill, and my way
of learning a change has been brought

to the state of my household affairs.
Let's be clear: I know what comes next.

Snap-crunch of the delicate bones of the world
in the well-designed jaws of the world

and being both worlds, both the cat and the mouse
(though it's likely a vole) and because like a god

or a demigod or simply by being a mind
and a body with two working hands

slipping peas from their pods at a sink,
I can exit this scene when the real business

starts. So I pull on my black rubber boots,
walk out through wet grasses, grateful for rain

which has finally come in the night. Huge storms
that have killed some, revived some, cracked open

the lives of some others. Late June. Wild cherries
dangle rain-shiny from rough-barked old trees.

Roses petal-less, thorny canes bent. Ditches
rushing with runoff, a suddenly wide creek

conveying what's dead to broad rivers downstream.
In the pasture, three willow trees shimmer and sigh.

I return to the kitchen to pick up the carcass, carry
what's left to the field, where I'll toss it, then get back

to work. Some days, like this one, there's nothing
at all to be found. No cat, not a scrap of the vole.

The whole room clean swept. As though
neither life happened, nor death. There's only

this morning sun warming wide empty planks
of pine floor and a bowl of shelled peas by the door.

The Way Back

You've washed your father's face
with a warm cotton cloth, lotioned his hands,

lifted his exhausted legs back into a narrow bed.
You've smoothed the sheets. He sleeps.

Return then to your chair by a wide window.
Watch a curved cup of moon slip

low in the west, glow creamsicle mango
as it touches the horizon's hard edge.

You are ten years old again, buckled
into the way back of a station wagon,

watching the world you are leaving
disappear into velvety black outlines

against deep blue. Your brothers and sister
asleep, curled around each other

in the middle seat. Someone speaking low.
You, apart, a slim slice of moon.

Like you are the only one left.
Like now. You looking backward.

Your father driving through darkness.
Both of you riding away.

Nightfall

In the small walled garden
of right now, a wild bird
keeps knocking its hollow
boned, richly feathered self

hard against a pane
gleaming in an old window,
the press of darkness
relentless, descends

on the luxuriant heads
of hydrangeas bent low
by heavy rain—this hour
when all sorrows are the same.

Some nights I step through different doors

onto different stone stoops and back porches,
pausing to wave to myself as I clack
slowly by on a train passing
into the outskirts of cities or small towns
through blank squares of blacktop
or freshly turned fields, and the self
that is moving waves back to the selves
that are stepping down into deep snow drifts
or dead grass or over discarded crack vials
or into a tiny, tilled spice garden vivid
with marigold, parsley, and mint.
The doors lead me back through the rooms
I once slept in, beds narrow or wide, windows
open to ocean or air shaft, two rooms
on two sides of a high bridge and one
with an ornate and worn-out unraveling carpet
of intertwined ivy and swans
where I told myself lie after lie.
I was here. And then here. And then here,
says the click of the rails, and I'm here,
riding past me and past me, again and again,
as though I'm a singular self, not a blur,
not a story that changes when memory
ticks by like a train in the night
pulling passenger car after car,
with their flickering lights and their shifts
of perspective, a face like my own
in each dark window frame.

Tightening the Trellis

When we transplanted raspberry canes
pulled wild from the hedgerows,
we tied them up with the uncoiled electrical guts

of an old boat trailer's brake lights,
looped plastic color-coded wires
post to post, with no need to think of circuitry

or poles or how current gets employed
to twist confession from the powerless,
our purpose only to give thorny sprays

a place to prosper, drape, to rest
their red and golden berries far from where
they first took root near ancient Troy.

Rubus idaeus. The story says a rose bush
on Mount Ida taught itself to transform blossoms
into sugared bodies made from sun, earth,

rain, build cups of sweetness
out of aggregated drupelets, offer sustenance
to every passerby—a trait not widespread

among humans. Or so the story goes.
Today, we watch the news, then tighten red, green,
yellow cords gone slack from winter's weight

with a twisting action that recalls
the root of torture—twist of elbow, wrist, or rack,
or wire on a cathode—simple tricks

to take apart a man. We can't escape
the things we know. Everything that's ever happened
is all here, every day. No matter what

we grow, how small a plot we till,
what walls we build, the world keeps showing up:
the wars, the boats, uprootings, conquest,

rape, how the knots that hold the harvest
also hold garrotte and noose. A feathery
spray brushes a not-yet saw-toothed leaf across

my hand—sweetness can be learned, the story
tells that too. Come back midsummer, you'll see then.
We'll sit in shade, eat all the berries that we can.

Pothole

Driving home last night, you swerved
the car to avoid a pothole—lurched hard
to one side—and I grabbed the door handle

remembering another car, another man,
another swerve but that one filled with menace
and his shouted words, *I can just end us now!*

as he jerked the car into oncoming lights.
How do any of us survive our loves?
That was years ago. The mind resolves

to forget, yet the body always remembers.
Outside was dark and overcast, the world
on its seesaw between winter and spring.

Memory's maw opens to swallow us
in every weather. We do the only thing
we can: hold tight to each other's hand.

The Story Their Way

Clio, Muse of History, walks with me morning
and evening, her nose to the air,

to the ground, through sweet corn and bean fields,

through pastures and steep-sided woods
packed with walnuts and cedar

as she follows the spiced earthy present tense only.

Not me: I'm ragged with news of the news
of what's happened and what is to come.

We crisscross the creek where she drinks

as I deal out fat sycamore leaves to the current,
watch them ride for the river, but mostly

they snag up, spin slowly in eddies,

and sink. We move on. Clio doesn't waste time
on the past. She knows what happened,

how everyone else tells the story their way.

She's a dog with no dog in the fight.
Not that she's blameless, just honest.

Sometimes, when I call her to walk,

she's stretched in the shade on a stone step,
licking her chops at the chicken house door.

Proverb

Gray-green patches of lichen
line up on the roof slates

like lacy rosettes on a satin sash
awarded for tenacity,

each a perfect color-match
to the splintered slats,

gray-green with age
on clapboard walls below.

Lucky are those who find home.
Luckier, those who learn to become it.

As It Is

Sometimes, I glance up and I see
the world as it is, complete:
taking the form of a tree,

or inky-eyed black-capped chickadee,
or a figure in a cherry-red scarf
crossing a sliver of street,

as if to remind me that everything
stands for everything else.
Dusk now. Winter. The world's a snowy

hillside sketched with shagbark hickories
and look—what I first thought
to be a string of small boats

on a white sea has turned into
a line of deer, following each other
single file, to take shelter beneath

boughs of big dark pines for the night.
That too seems exactly right.

How I Suit Up for Winter Storms

Boots from my son's eighth-grade year,
outgrown far faster than the heart-deep
humiliations he bore for being gay
that I could not protect him from.
I've worn them ever since through snow and sleet.
A sheepskin hat too hot for any weather
but what nor'easters scream down across fields,
one fleece edge turned so the bite
taken from it by our long-dead terrier mutt
is covered by the blue wool muffler
my daughter knitted for me
one fall when unemployed and anxious.
Leggings, snow pants, and here,
I might as well confess my underwear's
not good; it's functional, everyday,
won't ride up, which makes it perfect
for this task. Shirt, sweater, upscale
jacket passed down from a friend,
my husband's old coat with torn pocket,
bright red gloves my mother bought
on sale before she died, and zippered
in my sleeve's a chapstick and my father's
handkerchief. All set. I'm suited up,
armored, armed with shovel and salt,
to break and keep a path for any to come home.

II

Dominion

So close to understanding everything,
we lacked only a verb.

We had agency—
this was clear—why else would mists rise

                          to decorate the creek,
halo the river? Being water, we needed water—

so why else the rains, except to bless us,
                        fill our wells,

refill our sense of superiority?
We had been given dominion.

Spectacular landscapes
were designed as epic backgrounds for our rages

and desires, to lift our hearts
                            with our own grandeur.

This was known.
Only the verb was inscrutable.

                          Only the verb
stuck to the shadows, skittered outside

the circle of our fires,
eluded the grasp of our opposable thumbs.

             We had no idea
what to do, how to prove our dominion

                    except by ruining the world,
because that was our right.

                    So we ruined it.

Song for a Suburban Mid-Life Crisis

Four bedrooms, two baths.
Out front, a weeping cherry tree

and underneath each sink, a panoply
of poisons scented to the fantasy

of spotless linen hanging
sundried in an ocean breeze.

Don't get me wrong,
I've lived here too.

I've stood before an oval mirror
pulling tight the skin

above my ears to give myself
a temporary facelift,

watched my mouth
lose years of disappointment.

Even though I could not remember
what it was I wanted.

Grammar Lesson, Spring 2022

—conjugation is the variation of the form of a verb by which are identified the voice, mood, tense, number, and person.

Dead bodies *lie* in the road.
Dead bodies *are lying* in the road.
Dead bodies *were lying* in the road.
Dead bodies *lay* in the road.

Dead bodies *have lain* in the supermarket.
Dead bodies *have been lying* in the supermarket.
Dead bodies *had lain* in the supermarket.
Dead bodies *had been lying* in the supermarket.

Dead bodies *will lie* in the classroom.
Dead bodies *will have lain* in the classroom.
Dead bodies *will have been lying* in the classroom.
Dead bodies *will be lying* in the classroom.

Sentence Review:
Dead (*adjective*) bodies (*noun*) lie (*verb*)
in (*preposition*) the (*definite article*)
road /supermarket /classroom (*noun*)

Extra Credit: select the *dependent clause*
that contains unnecessary repetition:

hands bound behind backs/ shot through the head/
targeted for their color/ unidentifiable except by DNA/
again and again and again and again and again.

Choose Your Filter

A digital setting sun bronzes
our long, slender limbs, coronas

our faces with blazes of copper,
makes flames of our eyelash extensions

and manicured French tips,
anoints us with hot flares of honey-gold light,

so why wouldn't we think
we're the singular stars of the show?

Godlike, agleam, we can't take
our eyes off ourselves as we shimmer

and spark in this glamorous hour
before all goes dark.

Epiphany with Book in Hand

I slay flies by the score all morning,
great fat winter houseflies buzzing the window panes
facing south and I exaggerate
both time and body count—all morning, no,

but it sure feels like that—bumble and swat,
sweet silence, then a sudden batch of new
hatched flies appears for me to smack down
against the glass with *Stories That Could Be True*

by William Stafford—deeply contrary
to the spirit of his work, I realize,
his book held mid-air in the strange machinery
of my stranger hand. What a stack of lies I am.

All killer instinct, through and through.
But deep in marrow, these hot streaks of rue.

Lunacy

I battle a stuck window above the bathtub
on the first mild evening in April

after unrelenting cold by banging hard
on rails that held tight all winter long

with fists that held tight too.
I pound the weather-spattered sash

as if it were a rusted prison door that opens
into wildly temperate spring.

Turns out, it is.
The window gives.

Allows a quarter moon trailing its gauzy
negligee of light to float with me in warm water

as I listen to a congress of tree frogs
no bigger than shirt buttons

sing to the world born of rain in the ditches
to unclench its hands, begin over again.

Wheel (2)

Shiva, god of destruction, has taken my shape,
or I've taken his, the physics

        of embodiment being unclear to me,
          but not to the swallows in tailored blue jackets

swooping over the mower, as we cut down
the pasture, a thick haze of insects and chaff

        rising golden behind us, making Shiva
        and me the loud and benevolent

bringers of feast, our multiple arms
hard at work at the levers, birds

        bingeing above us and the day
        is a dance between air, earth, and force.

The best part is the start, when we make the first
turns back and forth with our crown of swift flyers,

        soft roaring of horsepower, headphone
        cords snaking our shoulders, the music

of spheres in our ears with the whir
of sharp blades in hovering circles below.

        We turn and we turn and we cut
        and we cut, making way for green shoots

of new grasses to grow. I watch for fawns breaking
from vanishing cover as we chop up their nurseries,

        destruction, creation, one side to the other,
        watch them head into woods-edge

and vanish. Foxes and vultures and hawks
watching too. We don't stop. We don't stop

        once we've started. We don't stop when
        the whir strikes a thick mass of straw grass

protecting a warren of rabbits, when Shiva holds
firm to the wheel as a terrible fountain

        of soft grey-brown bodies spews out
        of the earth, scattering in panic

or twitching where they lie on the ground.
Shiva tells me time isn't on anyone's side—

        we *are* time, we become it
        each day with our gigantic wheels

and our motorized scythes
spinning life into death into life

        into death and there's no turning back
        or aside. There's famine or feast, and today

is all feast. Swallows circle above us,
inscribing this text of the world in the sky.

Weeding After an Argument

Neither of us
talking.

Instead, we grip
living things

by their crowns,
rip their roots

satisfyingly
out of the ground.

World in Miniature

Sunny expanses
of buttercups edge

both sides of the tractor path
as yesterday's fresh

tadpole hatch bakes hard
in the skillet of a dried-up rut.

A Map of the Universe

> —*from the illustration in* The Principals of Philosophy, 1644

Like us, the map's a failure.
Descartes' diagram, certain as any theory,

etches the spinning paths of planets,
comets, sun, each body riding the puffed sail

of its singular vortex, shifting among
woven fabrics of unknown elements.

No explanation, but it looks really good.
It's left to us to resolve how chaos

rules despite such elegant design
and where's the fun in that?

No wonder we refine our cruelties,
explode in righteous indignation,

heft spike-studded clubs in the shape
of the stars and galaxies all spinning here.

Strangely beautiful, this failed idea.
Also, just like us.

The Uses of Grief

Mother, why did I think of you today
as I drove winding roads you never knew
in a place you never passed through?
Was it the dented detour sign
or one-way bridge, the dappled patch
of mayapple, the gravel shoulder's
crackle, or how our journeys veer unknown
so fast that made me pull off the road
to conjure you alive and in your beauty,
making me sixteen again and unafraid—
no knife yet at my throat, no belted
hands—just you alive again and me
beside you unencumbered by what's
demanded of a body to survive.
I sat you in the car and cried for you,
but really, I was grieving for the girl
I'd been, her lightness and her light.
You rode the detour with me, every turn,
until we found the main road where you
vanished once again. Again, I didn't
see you go. I was watching the azure
sky above us shimmer with exactly
the same deep blue as all the other thens.

Human Interest Story

Last bit of the newscast,
a tiny Tinkerbell-sized light
lifted from the dank bottom
of the jam-packed Pandora's Box
of horrors just unleashed at us
with shrieking chyron banners
and pop-up advertisements
for which heinous true crime story
or FBI procedural is coming up,
but for 30 seconds we see puppies
rescued from a storm drain,
a wedding ring returned
to a recent widow after fifty years
lost in a Nebraska cornfield, and yesterday,
a man with one arm paralyzed
was offered a simple loop
to bind his dead arm to his working one
in such a way that he could now
raise both arms above his head
in a ballerina's O, lift them over
his young son's body to hug him back,
and I can't stop seeing the look
on their faces, lit so brightly
from within, it's hauled me through
this whole next day on hope.

Spell

Unlikely find in a thrift store's back bin:
linen sheets that when washed and fitted

to my bed, felt so light I slept in them
as though I had become a gauzy net of spun flax

woven to so delicate a mesh that the weight
of every woe that had befallen me

had somehow fallen through me, dropped away
from me, magically, and none of it mattered.

I tell you this was fairy tale stuff.
I had no ragged edges whipstitched into worms.

No scars, no patches, scorch marks, burns.
I was part of everything, apart from nothing.

Yet when I woke, I woke afraid.
Now, what was I to do, walk out into the world

without my tragedies, without my griefs
packed into the long, drawn-out shadow

I'd dragged as ballast behind me, valiantly, for years?
Well, no need to worry: spells don't last.

Their beauty's in their brevity.
But sometimes, I can summon this one back,

when sheets are freshly washed and smoothed
across the bed—I close my eyes, lie

lightly in the weave, and for a moment,
I become a thousand sky-blue blossoms

floating in a field of flax,
unthreshed, unbroken, and unspun.

III

Warm Night with Storm and Moon

I sit out with my dog waiting for bats to appear
as the storm moves safely out to sea, according
to the weather on TV, storm clouds pulling east
in patterns that mirror the furrowed field below,
but aren't there people on boats out in that ocean?
And how does a storm move safely? It's a storm.
It can't hold handrails or step mindfully over
the wonky post office threshold no one has fixed
despite a general eagerness in the whole country
to litigate. My doctor asks: have you fallen recently?
I say yes, but not how you mean. I live on a farm.
I fall down all the time. Groundhog holes, ditches,
roots, cats, carelessness, that low door frame
in the corncrib because people used to be shorter.
A few bats skitter between maple and spruce
and a fat moon is now glamming up the last clouds
with a dramatic black-and-white chiaroscuro
that drowns out the delicate lights of fireflies
rising above the pasture's dark waves. So many
little boats out there. A small farm is a good life
if you could make a living. Even with subsidies.
Oh, hush now. Hush. Moonlight is shining all over us.
It's shining on my hands and legs, on the dog's
graying coat, shining on the wing flash of bats.
Moonlight is silvering our fence line, the barn's
tin roof, the ribbon of unlined road curving away,
the same road we take whether coming or going.
The world is doing its work on us. That's why
we sit out until bats appear, why we wait a moment

more before we rise to go inside. See, the sky's completely clear. Storm moving on. May it move, as it moves, slowly or swiftly, but may it move only across the waters of an unpeopled sea.

Awake

Into the spring-fed heart of the creek's
deep pool, I plunged,

my body a flame leaping through late-day heat.

I was jolted so awake
that all night I've felt the water

that held me in its cold green core

slip through slick stones
and sluices, tumble

into the slow, widening

riverbed, swirl beneath sycamore
branches rooting themselves

in sky, so I know, even now,

awake in morning's
milky light, that some of me

has already reached the sea.

Flight School

At first glance, I wonder what's dead
beneath the turning wings
of turkey vultures in a cloudless blue

but nothing's there. So, this
must be a day made all for play: buzzards
kettle and climb the warm columns

of air, then dive down to earth, one
by one, swoop and plunge,
soaring back on tight spirals of updraft

again. Creatures as certain
of gravity, matter, and aerodynamics
as I was, as a child, of the strength

of my father—who flew off
the known world last year—when he'd toss
my small body impossibly high

into sky and then catch me
as solid as lift, way back on the days
when he taught me to fly.

Digging a Dog's Grave

We take turns.

Even after a week of rains
a pickaxe is required.

We break the gravelly
crust, alternate spade
and shovel, open

a space for her body.

This is not the first grave
of a dog we have dug.

No telling if it's the last.

We know so little
of the ground beneath us.

Except how hard it is.

How right, on days like this,
that it's so hard.

Alchemy

The visible world
trembles
inside a water droplet
centered
in the ruffled wheel
of a lady's mantle's leaf

so I kneel,
tip the silver drop
into my palm,
let it ride
my finger
down

to fingertip,
drip back into
delicious
earth where
disappearance
means return.

Wheel (3)

Yes, I repeat myself. That's what I'm for.
Obsession is a turning wheel. Foxes
prowl the pasture, stalk fresh cut grass for mice
not from obsession, but design, because
the giant wheels of our newly paid-off
tractor have just crisscrossed the field, brush hog
attached—that time of year. Everything dies,
everything returns, everything repeats
itself. Almost the exact same mixture
of sea-blue chicory and Queen Anne's Lace
broadcasts its colors in the ditches, small
dark eyes skyward. I repeat, I repeat
myself: it's obvious we're all the same.
Design may be obsession's other name.

Waters Toward a Sea

Because the lever for the bathtub drain
has rusted shut with age, I wedge a finger

between ring and washer, pry up the plug
and the great guttural glug and swirl begins

the wild enthusiastic rush
as one small body of water races

for the ocean, days away, thrill-rides
the pipes' dark turns plumbed years ago,

knocks post and stud and mouse nest
made of chewed-up childhood quilts,

shudders past worn electric wiring,
and plunges down to cellar,

to the big-mouthed, clay-fired,
gray-water pipes, all the systems

of this whole house banging
their pots and pans to celebrate escape—

that's how I'd like to go out too—
with whoosh and clang

and gravity's insistent pull as I tumble
into other streams that pour off

culverts, creeks, and mountainsides,
all flowing toward the ocean,

which might be home,
or might be some symbolic stand-in for eternity,

or might simply be
the deep, unbounded, wide-open sea.

How This Bee Stuffs Its Pockets

There is a name for the color of pollen
this honeybee is packing into its thigh pouches
as it works the Mexican sunflowers
with exuberant purpose

and it's the name for the color of robes
worn by those who practice
detachment from worldly things,
a group that does not include me,

sitting back on my heels
in the wild summer garden
searching inside my head
for a word I can't remember,

or the bee, abdomen deep
in the actual bright center of a bloom.
I say turmeric, tangerine, marigold, ochre
but no door swings open.

I try apricot, butterscotch, amber.
Not it. The honeybee gathers
fat biscuits of pollen
the color of threads in a crocus' throat

or the orange-gold flecks in your eyes
when we met and I tumbled
in love with your eyes
flecked with saffron—oh, saffron's

the word that swings open a swoon
of first love. Now I'm both here
and there, in two places at once.
I'm saffron inside and out.

Ghazal for Summer Squash

At the end of every driveway, farm lane, garden gate
is a basket, bag, or pilfered milk crate labeled "free," filled with zucchini.

The female flower forms a yellow trumpet; the male's a thinner,
slightly duller bloom. Add a bee and we get more zucchini.

Loanwords are words adopted from one language and incorporated,
sans translation, into another: such as ghazal, sans, and yes, zucchini.

More potassium than a banana and only 25 calories makes
this charmer a nutritional powerhouse, says the PR lady for zucchini.

Julia Child served a dish called Tian de Courgettes au Riz,
composed of cheese, rice, too much work, and it's almost all zucchini.

One is a zucchina. But there's never only one. Perhaps a synonym
for surplus, surfeit, excess, glut, or way-too-much should be zucchini.

When possible, choose baby, small or barely medium, because
size matters when discussing gourds (and this goes double for zucchini.)

Shaved, dressed with garlic, panko, reindeer hearts or baco-bits,
blackened, sauteed, pureed, whipped to foam: it's still zucchini.

Love song for gardens, vines, and plenty, I raise a glass in praise
of final stanzas, to an end to this zucchini of zucchini.

Steady

One hour seated on the stone step
stroking the old dog's back from the tiptop
of her grizzled bony skull to her thin rump.

No brush, only my fingers, and lightly.
Soft tufts of gray-black fur fill my palm
each time, nest linings I cast to birds and wind.

She feigns sleep, nose-nudges my hand
when I stop. She's thirteen. It's August.
We play the game, stitched in our warm bodies

for this hour, silent and suspended,
as if the earth could hold itself steady,
take time to offer stillness, simple touch.

We'll lurch back soon enough to angle, tilt,
cold whirl of knowing what is to come.

Each Year

Each leaf argues
loudly in favor

of the crisp,
hard edges

of an individual
self as it skitters

down side streets
and farm lanes,

alone and in
mob rule

scaring up
shivering rackets

of sound
through back alleys,

re-spicing the air,
until finally,

finally, finally,
each softens

with weather,
gives over

its earth
to the earth.

Self-Portrait as Three Cubic Feet of Compost

That's three feet by three feet by three feet and will require a small truck to move, meaning I won't have that light-and-airy feel of ash, nor will I lift and vanish like a cloud ascending, *holy, holy, holy,* when cast to the winds as small odd-shaped bony bits clunk to the ground. I'll have heft. The brochure describes a layering of wood chips, alfalfa, straw, and me in a careful blend of nitrogen and carbon nestled inside a steel cylinder, then six weeks later: voila! Topsoil. Upside: no carbon footprint, no chemicals, no hot burn, because we've had enough of fires, haven't we? Downside: you can't just leave me in a drawer or on a closet shelf or sell me in my porcelain urn at a yard sale by mistake. I'll be work. You'll have to shovel me, so I suggest you simply dump me on the bigger compost heap and turn me for a season, then pay me out in spring to flower beds, red raspberries. Oh, to be threaded through with root, crisscrossed by traceries of vole and worm and grub! And what frisson thrills a thousand diamond points of frost and freeze may bring! By then, I'll be completely us/it/them/and/we. We'll germinate, get rinsed away, cling to a snowy egret's awkward yellow feet, fly, plummet, land, and settle back into the suck of black-gray mud. We'll collapse into cool dark corridors. We'll send up spiky stalks of pink-streaked lotus buds enclosing hearts made strange with chartreuse fruit and golden fringe. There'll be no end to us.

IV

Tricks of the Night Sky

How the sprawling vault of stars
appears to turn above us,

when it's us turning,
even when we know

it's us turning—
that's one trick.

Another is how I sometimes hear
your voice reminding me

which stars
along the ladle's edge point out

Polaris, north star, faint
but fixed, a trick

I listen for when lying out here
in the spin of it.

But it's the mirror trick
of distances that always does me in—

mad distances above,
mad distances within.

The Wisdom Package

I ask the youngish eye doctor why my eyes
itch and burn and new floaty bits
of paramecium-shaped debris swim through

my view each day, and he tells me
enthusiastically that this comes *absolutely free,*
with the wisdom package—an honor

I have been awarded. I blink. And, he adds,
the wisdom package comes with lots of other
free stuff too, but just like life, some people

will get more than others. I guess he's thirties,
forties tops, and I am falling in love with him
for his gentle way of reminding me I'm getting old,

and that it's a privilege. I've passed
the air-puff test, seen retinal scans which look
like the red-orange surface of the sun, each

with its pinprick dot of optic nerve—thin thread
connecting the eye to the dark, ornate theater
of the brain where the picture shows of our lives play.

I laugh and ask him about knees, knuckles,
liver spots, forgetfulness, and to each complaint
he answers: Wisdom! Wisdom! Wisdom!

We do not know one another's stories, how many
each of us has lost, the who or how of it,
from war, disease, or fate's unfairness doling out

more death to some than to others. He and I give
each other's hand a quick squeeze, let go,
and get back to the business of my sight.

He swings a heavy black heart suspended
from a giant arm in front of me,
clicks through pairs of lenses

with the careful ticks of a slowing clock.
I blink and answer him each time: clearer,
better, thank you, yes, much clearer now.

Some Silences Are Full and Deep as Wells

My brothers saw the northern lights
spiral into double helices,

glow neon green and twist above them
as they drove through a West Virginia night,

so they turned off the highway,
found a dark field where they leaned

against the warmth of a cooling engine,
watched the show.

They still talk about it sometimes.
When they do, a hush

falls over these two men, twins.
How it was just them and the lights.

Then it was just them.
And then they got back on the road.

Hidden Systems

A utility worker is being lifted into the air
        in a white bucket rising
        from a heavy truck

        where he meets another worker
swinging through the same air

        at the end of a different
        unfolding hydraulic arm

and they reach toward each other, touch,
        pass something
        between them—

        and isn't this how the intricate
machinery of circumstance

        works? Invisible
        crews on the ground, operators,

supervisors, invisible flaggers in hard hats who've set out
        bright orange cones
        changing the traffic's ebb and flow—

        Tell me, how many minuscule
and interlocking parts made possible

        our meeting in the wild currents
        of that city, that hour, that day?

These Mornings When

my whole heart beats
against the drumskin
of my body as though
a makeshift jazz
band has been jamming
all night long in me
and the tenor sax and bass
have only just now
slipped their instruments
into the soft velvet
insides of hard cases
and are riding the trains
home, tired, happy,
imaginary money
jingling in their pockets,
while the percussionist
taps out the last hi-hat
vibrations of my dream
into the turning world,
holding that quiet buzz
of having played well
all night, for each other,
even when there was no one
to listen, no one to applaud,
no one to throw a single
shiny coin into the hat.

Ode to the Bird on Edith Wharton's Hat

—from a photograph by E.F. Cooper

The hat that sat flat on her upright head
above the high-necked pearl-pinned blouse,
the leg-o'-mutton sleeves, above the two
long-haired chihuahuas seated on her silken
lap with silver bells around their charming
well-groomed necks—what iridescent
madcap blackbird dive-bombed down
into that neat, beribboned, tightly woven
world up there, leaving only its exotic
swallowtail as a stiff flag marking precisely
where it drove the arrow of its beak and body
into satin, skimmer, coif, and cranium,
to fill that sad-eyed head with gleaming
brilliant thoughts of flight? O bird!

How to Build a Castle

> —Henry Chapman Mercer, American archaeologist, tile maker,
> and designer of three "castles": Fonthill, his home, the Moravian
> Pottery and Tile Works, and Mercer Museum

Begin with earth, with mud, with clay,
begin with your child-hands

                that haven't yet learned to throw a fist.
                Begin palms flat and wide as the world

appears to be, then knead the earth
smooth, roll it, shape it into snakes

                to coil and pinch for pots to carry water,
                gather figs. From what else but earth

would we begin? Pat together sun-baked
mudpies, stack them into walls to make a house.

                (Abode comes from abide: a waiting place;
                the word adobe's from the Arabic for brick.)

Now build. Make walls and doorways,
tile the floors like Pompeii, cover vaults

                and columns with the Alhambra's
                interlocking patterns, fill a capitol

with tales of harvest, hunt, bees,
constellation, antelope, weasel, tree-song,

                tulip, hawk. Build hearths and mantels
                out of stories drummed and spoken

mouth to ear and ear to mouth, of what
was here before us, what we've built

                and what our building has destroyed.
                Cement what's disappearing into one

mosaic telling how we made ourselves
from what we had: earth, water, fire,

                these two hands. Tell that our making
                is the story. Tell how the story starts with clay.

Monotype

Ink the smooth glass plate
deep glossy black

and thick as moonlight's sheen on quiet water

etch a path through night fields
trace the line of a remembered cheek

reveal a face or landscape

                    by what's been taken from it.

Leave the sky dark
as an eye, the eye dark

as a sky, rich with mystery.

Lay on the paper.
Burnish the back.

For once, you decide what's wiped away.

Dear Tea Kettle

Oh, flat-bottomed, stainless-steel vessel,
black-handled, straight-sided, plain, no curlicues,

copper trim, goosenecks, or songbirds in flight—
you heat water for tea without drama

or heart-piercing horror film screams shouting
news of the boil, but instead, your subtle

raised lid sounds a glorious baritone note
building stately and slow to the three-layered chime

of a Norfolk and Western long bell steam whistle
that hums the bright rails of my rib bones awake,

makes my hot mug of oolong both journey
and transport on harmonic chords as

I move through the doorway of dawn
and onto the train of this day.

What I Learned Picking Blackberries at the Farm Dump

That a world filled with rusted tin cans and cobalt blue glass shards from old cold cream pots spins out

buckets of fat beaded globes fed by thunder and sun, fed by hot summer downpours washing down gullies through thickets of thorn.

That the thickets bear fruit atop great arching sprays on sharp-studded canes of the past.

That canes terrify flesh.

That some glossy berries are tight, bitter, juiceless, a mouthful of grit. That I spit these out.

That it's hard to know which ones are which until tested by tongue. By then it's too late—all that sour's inside.

But also—when perfect—the sweet's inside too.

That the thorns on the canes punish any resistance with barbed hooks curved back, drawing blood.

To escape you must reach deeper in.
That ticks live there too.

That calm is demanded and a rough long-sleeved shirt buttoned collar to cuff, canvas pants, heavy boots, and a coffee can hung on a string.

That the dark, richest berries need shade to grow sweet.

That they purple my hands as I pick, and they purple my mouth as I eat,
and they purple this jam cooked with sugar and lemon

pried open in winter and spooned out on toast

with the purple of all of it:
present, past, body, blood, bittersweet, heat, rust, and sky.

This Late Thanks

Hickory nuts shake down from shagbarks
onto blacktop, their leather cases cracked

at the seams, releasing the dense center
that as a child, I'd try to bust open for food

with a hammer against stone. It never worked.
My first careful blows revealed an intricate

chambered hardness that clenched the meat
too tightly for my fingers to pick out

so I'd bring the hammer down hard as Thor,
and smash the halves to mush shot through

with broken shell, impossible to eat.
Sometimes, a truck's weight can't bust

a hickory nut's core. Today, they drop
atop the asphalt, or skitter into ditches

where they'll soften and take root,
get storm-washed into creeks to rot, decay,

go round again. For years, I thought
I could discover where the sweet spot lives

between swift obliteration and slow patient time—
the angle, pressure point, the perfect words

to pry wide the small hard architectures
we hold so tight inside—but no such place.

Instead, I have this late and quiet thanks
for fate or happenstance or even grace,

that any one of us has fallen, broken just enough,
onto an earth, or into hands, that give.

Wheel (4)

There is a *how* to it but not a *why*,
    we know enough to know that much, not more,

        but I repeat myself. That's what I'm for.
    Obsession is a turning wheel. Fox prowl

the way tree roots upturned are birds flown into sky
    as if the point is to become what we are not—

        not by obsession, but design, because
    we know enough to know that much, not more.

In early spring our footsteps green the path,
    the giant wheels crisscross the field

        the swallows swoop and dive
    as if the point is to become ourselves

and then, in time, an otherness that dies, returns,
    repeats itself in early spring. Almost

        the same blue chicory and Queen Anne's lace
    green the path we've walked together

through tall woods, which is an otherness
    we will become in time, because we *are* time,

        we become it, dark eyes skyward
    as everything around us wheels and turns.

Design may be obsession's other name
        and I repeat myself: that's what I'm for.

        We're all the same; we turn around that core
        as swallows write this text into the sky:

There is a *how* to it but not a *why*.
        We know enough to know that much, not more.

Acknowledgments

Grateful acknowledgment is given to the editors of the following publications where these poems first appeared, some in altered form.

American Journal of Poetry: "Digging a Dog's Grave," "Miniature World," "Waters Toward a Sea"

Baltimore Review: "Monotype"

Bracken: "Tightening the Trellis" (as "*Rubus Idaeus*") "Wheel (1)"

Broadkill Review: "How This Bee Stuffs Its Pockets"

Cave Wall: "Ode to the Bird on Edith Wharton's Hat"

diode: "I Go for A Walk While My Cat Eats a Mouse," "Some nights I step through different doors"

The Dodge: "Dominion," "Nightfall"

The Lascaux Review: "Falling" (as "Confession")

Neshaminy: "How to Build a Castle"

One Art: A Journal of Poetry: "Ghazal for Summer Squash," "Human Interest Story," "Lunacy," "Song for a Suburban Mid-life Crisis," "These Mornings When," "This Late Thanks, " "Weeding After an Argument"

Plume: "Spell"

River Heron Review: "Grammar Lesson, Spring 2022," "The Way Back"

Schuylkill Valley Journal: "Awake," "Pothole," "Some Silences Are Full and Deep as Wells"

Southern Poetry Review: "Here," "Warm Night with Storm and Moon," "Wheel (2)" (as "Shiva, God of Destruction, Mows the Pasture with Me")

The Sun: "The Wisdom Package"

Thrush: "Self-Portrait as Three Cubic Feet of Compost"

U City Review: "Flight School," "The Story Their Way" (as "Clio, Muse of History"), "What I Learned Picking Blackberries at the Farm Dump"

Vox Populi: "How I Suit Up for Winter Storms"

"Grammar Lesson, Spring 2022" received a 2023 Pushcart Prize.

Thank you to Cheryl Bomba for the use of her photograph, "Staying the Course," and to Diane Lockward for her editorial guidance. Thank you to the Pinkers, Worders, and others who have thoughtfully encountered these poems along the way. As always, thank you to Reb, Sam, Abby, Seth, and all those whose footsteps have greened the path through tall woods with me.

About the Author

Hayden Saunier is the author of five previous collections of poems, most recently *A Cartography of Home* (Terrapin Books, 2021). Her awards include a 2023 Pushcart Prize, the 2013 Gell Poetry Award, the 2011 Rattle Poetry Prize, and the 2011 Pablo Neruda Award. Her work has been published in such journals as *Beloit Poetry Journal, Nimrod, Southern Poetry Review, The Sun,* and *Virginia Quarterly Review*. Her poems have also been featured on *Poetry Daily, The Writer's Almanac,* and *Verse Daily*. A professional actor, she is the founder and director of No River Twice, a community-driven interactive poetry group that combines poetry and performance. She lives on a farm in Pennsylvania.

www.ingramcontent.com/pod-product-compliance
Lightning Source LLC
Chambersburg PA
CBHW030531080526
44586CB00011B/395